MW00982069

I CAN BE ME

An Inspirational Coloring Book For All Ages

First Edition Copyright **978-1-300-35736-0**

I CAN BE ME© by Jean Handley 2012. All rights reserved.

Front Cover Image: WELL, WISE, WORTHY, WEALTHY
an original quilt by the author
Cover Design, Back Cover image and Book layout by B.A.Callahan
Cover Image Photography by Mark Frey

Dear reader
Enjoy the poems
Do as you please
Reading, discussing, learning, coloring,
All create new realties.

I CAN BE ME

It is customary when writing a book
To thank those whose time I gratefully took.
My gratitude goes to my mirrors: Ram and JZ,
Winsor, Bev, Victoria, Barbara, Carol and Teri,
Jean, Joe, Trena, John and Katina,
Miceal, Christine, Bettye and Julie,
My much loved friends and family;
And all of RSE.

With the clarity of poetry
The words burn bright
From consciousness they alight.

I CAN BE ME

How does one change
When living in a bind?
Open a book
Open your mind.

I CAN BE ME

I sat in a garden so lovely.
I observed a busy buzzing bee.
With radiance the flowers glowed
Their bounty overflowed.

I CAN BE ME

The waves came into shore singing
Hi diddle dee dee
Then departed back into the sea.
I played in the sand.
With the ocean, we struck up a band.
I CAN BE ME

An event began my quest.
Wave function ignited the crest.
The quantum world became decree.

I CAN BE ME

When a thought makes me cry
The wind blows erasing the tears dry.

I CAN BE ME

I climbed a tree. It sent leaves on a spree.
What a large oak, "Welcome" it spoke.

I CAN BE ME

I dreamed of sovereignty
Everything from A to Z.
Materials needs met, I was all set.

I CAN BE ME

Into deep space I flee
My arms in a Vee.
I spread them wide, stars at my side.

I CAN BE ME

Into midbrain I go
New roads of consciousness to hoe.
I train my sight, my future is bright.
There is so much I can do with remote view.

I CAN BE ME

Challenges can seem so alarming
Doing away with what is known
Peeling to reveal the inner self is disarming
But it is what I have to own.

I CAN BE ME

The caterpillar eats green leaves
Crunch, crunch, crunch
It is always having lunch.
One day boredom moves it to change
Into something very strange.
A cocoon is its fate, emergence it does await.
Transmutation is taking place, its past it does erase.
A butterfly is born anew with wings of brilliant hue.

I CAN BE ME

Unbridled emotion can rave and rant
But laser sharp focus maintained in a chant
Is not sophomoric, it can become a harmonic.
The repetitive stance produces a trance.
A neuronet is created
A reality is obligated.
I CAN BE ME

I marched into the forest full of expectancy.
It is a place made of harmony.
Even the fallen limb makes a home for kin.

I CAN BE ME

In many lives judgment is a measure
Good/bad, beautiful/ugly, victim/tyrant.
But when we still those emotions
Retract - not react
Joy becomes our greatest treasure.

I CAN BE ME

I slid on a rainbow laughing yippee
I spun all through the colors merrily.
The spectrum of light
Was made with raindrops in delight.

I CAN BE ME

I love learning
My fingers turning page after page
Bringing tales of an ancient sage
Stories of wars that once did wage
Knowledge of particles from complex to minute
Photos of landscapes and of puppies so cute.
It does enthrall. I embrace it all.
I CAN BE ME

We went for a walk
An afternoon of fun and talk.
With my turtle, dog and cat
Under a gnarled willow tree we sat.
Each had a soliloquy.

I CAN BE ME

I observed a laboratory filled with chemistry
I saw with my own eyes a lot of frequency.
I asked with the respect of a knave,
"Is my chair a particle or a wave?"

I CAN BE ME

The unified field theory
Is not such a mystery.
I create a picture of my dream
Observing it intently
Combining gravity and electromagnetism
Triggers my idea into reality.

I CAN BE ME

I dove under the sea.
Who'll play with me?
A shark gave me a race
In between seaweed that looked like lace.

I CAN BE ME

I saw a magnet in action,
Each pole had a reaction.
The center is the alignment without damaging,
emotional excitement.
I have no past. I have no future.
I am free at last.
Oh wow! I can live in the now!

I CAN BE ME

Into the earth I placed a seed.
I dreamed it would grow very fast indeed.
Everyday I did spy
Encouraging it to try and try and try.

I CAN BE ME

I think a genius is someone whose creativity is almost continuous.
They are rarely caught without a thought.
To bring dreams into reality though
Takes a pause
Surrender is one of the universal laws.

I CAN BE ME

I tried to be hip, I tried to be cool
I tried to be pretty, romantic and skinny.
I ended up a fool.
So I embarked outside my comfort zone
Creating new goals of genius, health and love.
The future is now mine to hone.

I CAN BE ME

The midnight blue sky filled me with rapture
The glistening lights I wanted to capture.
I talked to a star, who answered me from afar.

I CAN BE ME

The smoke rises in a design
My thoughts entwine.
My pipe is a tool
That stops the swing of the dual.
The nitrous oxide rewires the nueronets
With ideas I had not contemplated yet.
I CAN BE ME

The helicopters fly
From the maple trees in the sky.
They land upon the earth,
Next Spring to give birth.

I CAN BE ME

I held my nose to a delicate rose
The petals reflect the unfoldment of self
Life's bounty, its experiences, its wealth.
It's all I want to be.

I CAN BE ME

With my deck of cards, I play hide and seek.
I try to remote view
But sometimes, I peek.
Someday, maybe, the joker will teach me poker.

I CAN BE ME

I skippered a boat, turned hard to lee
The wind in my face brought such glee.
We came about, a whale did spout.

I CAN BE ME

I sat at twilight, gazing into the sky.
Entities and orbs appeared,
They say hello and goodbye.
Their colors and sizes do vary.
I like it when they tarry.

I CAN BE ME

The music starts pounding
The energy abounding
And when I dance, I fall into a trance.

I CAN BE ME

The snowflakes softly fell.
They put me into a spell.
Whoever invented a blizzard
Surely must be a wizard.

I CAN BE ME

We all have a polka dotted past
Stories we revel in
Stories when we have committed sin.
To break these bad bonds
I raise my hand in confession
Erasing the shame and guilt
I move into the future with the learned lesson.
I CAN BE ME

I climbed a mountain, I had to be hardy.
It reached the sky without boundary.
To a passing cloud I embraced
"Hello," out loud.

I CAN BE ME

There are many a story
Of adventure, wealth and glory.
They are attributed to yesteryear...
but they are here.
Giants, elves and fairies and more
With opened eyes can be seen today
Those of lore.

I CAN BE ME

When I am feeling befuddled
Everything around looks muddled.
I pause and ask myself consciously
How can I turn this into an opportunity?

I CAN BE ME

I was caught in ignorance, a hidden wedge
Till science presented knowledge.
Everything I needed, I did find
Truth filled my mind.

I CAN BE ME

Angel's wings are quite beautiful things
They move with grace and poise.
Wrapping 'round my heart
When comfort is needed
Expanded wide to celebrate joys.

I CAN BE ME

My desire is to have dominion over my life spiritually,
Creating my day, focusing on the future.
Though it is an alone journey, I do it
While maintaining community with humanity.
I am resolved to live evolved.

I CAN BE ME

The frogs croaking chorus
Are singing for us.

I CAN BE ME

The tulips on their stems sway
They bloom in Spring and for a while stay
Till they hit their peak and then die away.
"We believe in reincarnation," they say.
"We'll be back another day."

I CAN BE ME

I searched for earthworms under a tree
They must be napping catching many a Zeee...
I eavesdropped moving underground
The earthworms never made a sound.

I CAN BE ME

The subconsciousness mind is a library
With focus, it is a laser in a quarry.
It reveals itself when called upon
For anything...
science, time travel or a simple yarn.

I CAN BE ME

The true purpose of wine
Is to bring out the divine.
The nitrous oxide makes nueronets movable
Even making people you do not like, lovable.

I CAN BE ME

With my body I have so much fun,
I slide and twirl and climb and run.
I sure do giggle when I wiggle.

I CAN BE ME

I played a game, not of serendipity
But a choice of liberty.
It is not hocus-pocus.
It is focus.

I CAN BE ME

A spider I can tell
Weaves webs very well.
In the ultraviolet field
Radiant health it does yield.

I CAN BE ME

Some people look upon
Writing poetry as an experience quite humble.
I enjoy the puzzle letting the words tumble and jumble.
Let them play, fumble, even stumble.
Let them ring with laughter, not a mumble.
And to conclude, with a flourish,
Let me add a B for bumble.

I CAN BE ME

My candle is a tool
To move my brain from hot to cool.
I stare into the flame
My thoughts it does tame.

I CAN BE ME

I observed an ant, though he worked very hard
He never did pant.
With all his friends they built a fort of a sort.
So I made a goal, I dug a hole
I burrowed a new facility.
It felt comfy and cozy.

I CAN BE ME

There are beings in the unseen
Who are here to help, they are not mean.
Like a huge chorus, they are rooting for us.

I CAN BE ME

The great white silence fell all night.
When morning came it made a beautiful sight.
The snow and the winds did howl
A cathedral was made of many a tree bough.
The moment held such grace
Dark branches dressed with lace.
It felt like an eternity.

I CAN BE ME

My greatest desire is to be whole
Fulfilling the desire of my soul.
Each life allows another look
Involution and evolution
Chapters of a book.

I CAN BE ME

A penguin sure does have a lot of kin.
They waddle on ice, thick or thin.
But in the water, they look like a torpedo
in a tuxedo.

I CAN BE ME

Just surrender is now common advice.
But how is that implemented?
Quieting the mind, staying focused on a thought
Changes what agony might have wrought.

I CAN BE ME

A tornado is rotating wind in a fury
Moving from start to finish in a hurry.
If this twister were situated in the sky,
It would be a wormhole
Sucking matter into bye-bye.

I CAN BE ME

I chose to engage a labyrinth.
At its completion I knew I had changed
herewith.
I declare, I am free of being willy-nilly.

I CAN BE ME

Can I safely pass putting my foot on the gas?
Is that Joan on the phone?
Is there a line at the loo?
I don't have to have a clue.
I can know with remote view.

I CAN BE ME

The four bases found in DNA
Adenine, cytosine, guanine and thymine
Are in us all, small or tall,
No matter our color of skin, fat or thin.
We all have free will to take action or to be still.
We all walk the path to point zero,
Each of us is a human hero.

I CAN BE ME

Nature really knows how to recycle.
It burns wood for warmth as embers glow,
It takes rain and makes it snow,
It absorbs seeds into soil,
And watches them grow.
Even thoughts I borrow from the quantum field,
I return after using their knowledge revealed.

I CAN BE ME

Superstrings are such tiny things.
As the first piece of matter
They can become anything.
There are lines and circles and membranes,
That shimmy and bounce and twirl.
And though strings are still theory,
Eventually, I think, each one becomes a pearl.

I CAN BE ME

Shopping is so hectic, the energy is very kinetic
Slashing prices, big markdowns
Super bargain, all sales jargon.
I did get some towels though
A bag and makeup
And boots for the snow.
It's all a part of my creativity.
I CAN BE ME

Big black birds sitting on telephone wire,
Look like a church choir in funny attire.

I CAN BE ME

The toaster is set.
Did you think I would forget?
Plate, bread and knife
Each morning of our married life.
The designer jelly you always did cajole about,
Have I left anything out?
Wish you were still keeping me company.

I CAN BE ME

A little fir tree into the soil was new,
For many years it grew and grew,
Till one winter it was chosen,
Taken from the field still frozen.
On Christmas day, its dream had manifest...
It was dressed in a family's best.

I CAN BE ME

Light did shimmer looking into my mirror.
What did I see looking back at me?
The hidden host
That I love the most.

I CAN BE ME

Glossary

abounding - without boundaries

adenine - one of four bases for DNA

afar - at a distance

alignment - arranged in correct position

ancient - really old

anew - again

attributed - belongs to

beings - entities or other "people"

befuddled - confused thoroughly

bind - predicament

bough - branch

boundary - limit

bounty - generousness

burrowed - to dig

cajole - laugh lightly

clarity - clearness

chemistry - study of atomic and molecular stuff

cocoon - silky sleeping bag for a changing caterpillar

complex - intricate or a lot of parts

consciously - with self awareness

consciousness - state of awareness

contemplated - observed thoughtfully

creating - responsible for it to exist

crest - highest point

customary - usual practice

cytosine - one of four bases for DNA

decree - order or law

dedication - commit

departed - retreated or returned

disarming - becoming powerless

divine - god like

DNA - deoxyribonucleic acid - carries genetic information

dominion - complete responsibility

dual - two sides

electromagnetism - magnetism produced by an electric current

embarked - to start a journey

emergence - moving out of something

engage - participate

enthrall - captivate

entities - something or someone that exists as a separate being

entwine - twist together

eternity - no time, forever

evolved - growing, owning it all

evolution - journey from mass to point zero

expectancy - anticipation

facility - house

focus - core of concentration

frequency - a lot of wave functions moving around

genius - extraordinary intellect or talent

gnarled - misshapen or twisted

gravity - pulls two forces together

guanine - one of four bases for DNA

harmonic - acoustical frequency

harmony - happy agreements

hectic - really busy

helicopters - colloquial shaped leaves from a maple tree

herewith - right now or immediately

hocus pocus - meaningless words in magic

hoe - break through

hone - sharpen

host - master or spirit

hue - color

ignited - fired

image - personality

implemented - put into effect

involution - journey from point zero to mass

jargon - a language or slang

judgment - criticism

kinetic - in motion

knave - real troublemaker

labyrinth - maze

laser - specific focus or beam of light

lee - away from the wind

liberty - freedom or independence

loo - slang for toilet

lore - anecdotal or storytelling past

magnet - metal body that attracts iron or steel

manifest - dream came into reality

matter - physical being

measure - sizing up

membranes - two dimensional strings shaped like sheets

midbrain - psychic region of the brain

mind - result of consciousness and energy acting on the brain

minute - really tiny

mirrors - people who reflect me, back to me

muddled - confused

nitrous oxide - a gas

neuronet - nerve cells that work together or apart in the brain

obligated - compelled

observe - look at without distractions or focus on

opportunity - favorable time to open a door

orb - ball of energy

own - admit responsibility for

particle- smallest amount or when the wave function stops, it is a particle

pause - temporary rest

pole - opposite ends of a magnet

polka dotted - spotty

poise - balance

quantum - the smallest amount of something

quantum field - all things potentially, unconditionally

quarry - stone pit

quest - mission

radiance - brightness

radiant - brilliant or luminous

reality - what I create/think becomes my life

reincarnation - the soul living lifetime after lifetime

remote view - seeing the invisible using midbrain

resolved - determined

retract- withdraw or pull back

reveal - show or disclose

revel - to enjoy greatly

rewires - rearranges

sage - storyteller

serendipity - lucky accident

shimmer - glowing faintly

sight - the power of seeing

situated - located

skippered - master of a ship

soliloquy - expressing thoughts with yourself spoken aloud

sophomoric - intellectually immature

soul - book of your life

sovereignty - being independent

spectrum of light - distribution of colors

spree - moving in all directions

spirituality - all encompassing

subconsciousness mind – housed in the brain, attuned to the wisdom of the ages

superstrings - theory of the first and teensy pieces of matter

surrender - yield

tales - stories

tarry - stay longer

theory - best guess to explain something

thought - building block of the mind

thymine - one of four bases for DNA

train - focus

trigger - causes a reaction

trance - quieted mind, focused mind

transmutation - changing form

ultraviolet field - field of frequency

unbridled - not restrained

unfoldment - spread or open out

unified field theory - or theory of everything is an attempt to combine the big and small of relativity and quantum, solved by some say, superstring theory

unseen - other dimensions

universal law - like attracts like

wage - rage on or take place

wave - frequency moving up and down

wave function - particle in motion

wedge - block

willy-nilly - silly

wizard - magician

wormhole - space-time tunnel that joins dimensions

wrought - become

yarn - story

yesteryear - time past

zero point - the beginning, vacuum energy for all fields